FORD CARS

1945-1964

Alan Earnshaw
& Robert Berry

Nostalgia Road Publications

CONTENTS

THIS BOOK IS DEDICATED TO THE MEMORY OF
NORMAN BERRY
(1926-1980)

The **Nostalgia Road** Series ™

is produced under licence by

Nostalgia Road Publications Ltd.
Units 5 - 8, Chancel Place
Shap Road Industrial Estate, Kendal LA9 6NZ
Tel. 01539 738832 - Fax: 01539 730075
e-mail: sales@nostalgiaroad.co.uk

designed and published by
Trans-Pennine Publishing Ltd.
PO Box 10, Appleby-in-Westmorland, Cumbria, CA16 6FA
Tel. 017683 51053 Fax. 017683 53558
e-mail: admin@transpenninepublishing.co.uk

and printed by
Kent Valley Colour Printers Ltd.
Kendal, Cumbria 01539 741344

© Trans-Pennine Publishing Ltd. 1996 & 2004
Photographs: Ford of Gt. Britain or as credited

Front Cover: *The Ford Cortina model in all its various forms was to endear itself to generations of motorists and thus proved to be one of Britain's most successful cars of all time.*

Rear Cover Top: *This Prefect E493A model was one of the first Ford models to feature flush-fitting headlamps.*

Rear Cover Bottom: *Ford finally found their way through the period of post-war austerity and entered a new motoring era with an emphatic statement with the introduction of their MkI Consul and Zephyr models in 1950. With their trans-Atlantic styling and stunning looks, they were a big difference to the pre-war models.*

Title Page: *Early 8 and 10 horse-power cars nearing the end of the production line at Dagenham in the balmy pre-automation days.*

This Page: *The company founder, Henry Ford.*

ISBN 1 903016 69X
British Cataloguing in Publication Data
A catalogue record for this book is available from the British Library

INTRODUCTION

It is now some seven years since we launched the Nostalgia Road series, with a range of comprehensive but modestly-priced books on the history of British motoring. Today our range has extended to include trams, railways, tractors, and much more. Yet the most exciting period in the history of British transport has to be the 20 years that followed the end of World War II, for such was the momentous nature of change.

In this time we witnessed the nationalisation of road haulage and railways, along with a growing 'national-ownership' stake in bus operations. Yet by 1952 a change of government had reversed the moves towards integrated transport policies and granted greater freedoms to road users and by the mid-1950s, Henry Ford's dream of 'motoring for the masses' had become a reality.

Above: *The pre-war scene at Dagenham as a Model 62 with a 22hp V8 engine rolls off the assembly line. This would have been representative of the way Ford products would have been built between 1937 and 1939.*

The story in the demise behind our national railway system and the growth in the road network is told in our book *Steam For Sale*, but briefly put, the Conservative government of the day preferred road transport over railways. It therefore promoted two reports, one by John Buchannan who favoured growth in private car ownership and the development of super highways (motorways), and one by Richard Beeching that foresaw the mass closure of railway branch lines and local stations. It goes without saying that the main beneficiaries of this shift in transport philosophy could only be the motor manufacturers of Great Britain.

Ford's first factory at Trafford Park, Manchester

Model T 1914

Model T 1917

Model T 1923 - Fordor tourer

By the 1960s the affordability of private motoring had reached the working classes, and soon people turned their backs on public transport. Vehicles like the Austin A35, the Ford Anglia, the Morris 1000 and the Vauxhall Viva revolutionised the concept of private car ownership, and this led to the motor car becoming what is perhaps the most significant singular influence in our lives today. Even people who do not own a car will readily admit that the freedom of greater mobility that car ownership brought after World War II, has shaped the way of both our society and our social development today.

Indeed, the advent of car ownership has geared society to live at a much faster pace; it has also provided the criminal element of our race with a greater means of escaping detection and punishment. Whatever the case, the car is here to stay, but it also now has a firm place in our heritage too. For instance, who amongst us will ever forget their first car? Not only do we remember it in general terms, but more than likely we will also recall every minute detail about it as well.

Today car ownership is common and most households have at least one, but more frequently two and three cars per house are becoming the norm. Yet it is not that long ago that car-ownership was a luxury, and within living memory many of us recall that the only way to get around was by bus, train or on foot.

The achievement of car-ownership as a measure of 'social standing' was, in no small way, due to the progressive policies of the larger manufacturers and here in Britain firms like the British Motor Corporation, Ford, the Rootes Group and Vauxhall did more than their share of making this dream of utopia come to fulfilment. In the following chapters we look at the way in which Ford helped the 'common man' achieve his dream, by producing models that were both economical to buy and reliable in performance. In the post-war years Ford of Great Britain built on the traditions of mass-production and keen pricing that they had achieved in the earlier decades, and by models like those pictured in this introductory chapter.

For the majority of people the car meant ease in getting to and from work, or holidays and day trips into the country or to the seaside. It also created the previously unknown phenomena of traffic jams, particularly on Bank Holidays as the industrial towns and cities teemed out their masses on the seaside resorts like Brighton, Blackpool, Southend and Scarborough - how we recall Tadcaster and Malton on the A64 to the latter of these places. Winding roads through the Yorkshire Dales, the Lake District and the West Country were choked, and the market towns en-route became bottlenecks that often took more than an hour or so to pass through. Places like York on the A64, Taunton and Tavistock on the road west and Crawley and Reigate on the A23 came to be major bottlenecks, but perhaps the worst of the lot was the A6 with infamous delays at Buxton, Preston, Lancaster and Kendal.

So it came to be, that the words 'by-pass' and 'motorway' first began to be used in the English language - every major town it seemed wanted a by-pass, so contradictory to the earlier trends of taking all the roads through the town centre to capture trade. The first of these was the Preston By-Pass that opened in 1959 and became Britain's first section of 'motorway', now part of the M6. Those who were drivers or passengers in those days will no doubt recall the great traffic jams that bedevilled our road network in pre-motorway days. For some it was the towns of the Great North Road, or Penrith on the A6, with its notoriously narrow section between Devonshire Street and Middlegate.

For others it was the interminable slog down to the West Country, particularly between Bristol and Exeter, which occasioned conditions where frustrated fathers would have to quieten fractious children. Games like 'Count the buses', 'I-Spy', and 'See how many different types of car you can count' became part of the way of life to children of the 1950s and '60s.

Both of your authors were well aware of Ford's products in this era as such cars figured largely in our childhood. In Robert's case the family car was one of the old upright models, a Prefect E493A (JDK 807). Even years after its roving days were done, the old car sat in a corner of a field on the family farm providing shelter for the hens, and an adventure playground for the Berry children. Robert's childhood is also filled with memories of his uncle's Squire estate car, which ran beautifully for several years and took them on many excursions. Robert has also spent more time than he cares to recall on the restoration of two MkII Consuls, one a Highline model and one a Lowline model.

My 'Ford experience' came with an Anglia 105E Super (1604 NA), which finally arrived in August 1961 after we had endured the infamous waiting lists for 11-months. The Anglia lasted two years and was eventually replaced with a Consul Classic (76 VMB), of 1962 vintage. Though second-hand, this was one of the batch with which Ford had suffered so many teething problems. In fact, when my father bought it as a one-year-old car for £300 it had just 121 miles on the clock, plus a factory-fitted replacement 1500cc engine that was barely run in. It came to a sticky end when it met head-on with a National Coal Board wagon of Foden origin on a foggy September morning in 1967; fortunately this altercation took place directly outside the front gates of Doncaster Royal Infirmary.

Our replacement was UVH 21 a 1963 model of the Classic, though converted as a Lotus Classic and not actually put onto the road until January 1965. This rare beast came to us with just 1,239 miles on the clock, having only ever seen the interior of various Ford showrooms; though it had been entered in one race. It too came to a grievous end, one from which my fiancé (now my wife) and I were lucky to escape unscathed when it suffered a simultaneous rear-tyre blow-out at Leicester Forest East on the way back from the Wembley Assembly in July 1969.

From the outset then, this book will be a real Nostalgia trip for both the authors and hopefully our readers too. It is designed to look at Ford's products during the era, but also remind us of a time when cars in general had both character and individuality. As well as the new car showroom agencies, this was also the era of the back-street used car lot. In such back-street establishments you could be sure of finding almost anything, ranging from the mundane pre-war family saloons to exotic American saloons or continental cars that varied in their style and quality.

This post-war era was also the time when you could buy a used car and drive away in sure confidence; the sure confidence that the 'guarantees' of some salesmen meant nothing! Most were decent businessmen, but others were frankly little more than spivs. Alarmed at the proceedings of some of these back-street traders, the motor manufacturers and the reputable dealers established customer care programmes and training schools for the people employed in promoting, selling and repairing their models. This was an area in which Ford of Britain took an important lead and also excelled!

For many working class families, this was a period when they made a transition from the bus queue or railway platform to the Triumph, Velocette or BSA motorcycle. Dad would drive the 'bike to work on weekdays, and on a weekend or for the holidays they would add a side-car combination to transport the family and their luggage. From these they often went on to putting down their deposit for a little Austin or a 'Sit-Up-And-Beg' Ford! This was a time for the home mechanic, and washing the car in the drive ready for the weekend's motoring. The roads were still free of heavy traffic and petrol was relatively inexpensive, although considerable extra duty would be placed on fuel during and after the Suez Crisis of the mid-1950s. Yet, even this did not daunt the desire for private transport, and during the 1950s UK car sales increased significantly.

Model T 4 door saloon 1923

Model A Tourer 1932

Model A Saloon 1932

Model A Drophead coupe 1932

Model B 1932

Model Y Popular 1933

V8 30HP 1934

V8 30HP 1936

At the other end of the scale, there was the supreme elegance of a Rolls Royce whilst some owners, like the ostentatious and flamboyant Lord and Lady Docker with their customised Daimlers, went to extreme lengths of fashion. However, to the man in the street, these cars seemed a world away and as we will see later, Ford was ready to provide an affordable alternative. It was also an era where motor-sports became even more popular, and few could fail to be thrilled by the exploits of Messrs Hawthorne, Moss, Collins and other schoolboy heroes at the racing circuit. The Monte-Carlo Rally, the ultimate saloon car endurance race of the day, was there for almost anyone who wanted to 'Have-a-Go', provided they had the money of course! For younger enthusiasts, it was a time when every small boy began to know his cars, either from his I-Spy books or from the Dinky Toy catalogue.

Few European cars were on Britain's roads and of those that were there, most went unnoticed for they were not the commonplace sight they are today! However, a few models were just starting to make in-roads, especially the Renault Dauphine from France and the Volkswagen Beetle from Germany, whilst the land of gondoliers and ice-cream men offered us the Fiat!!! Talking of ice cream vans, this was a time children learned to be wary of the increased traffic on the road, especially when walking slowly back from an ice-cream van! As raspberry sauce dripped onto little fingers, policemen tried to get across the message 'Mind That Child'.

As these officers stood sentinel outside parks, schools and on street corners, their cars would be parked at the roadside. Their new patrol cars invariably would, without doubt, have been big, black and British; Austin, Ford, Riley and Wolseley being amongst the most common makes employed by the guardians of the law, who were rapidly making the change from push-bikes or flat feet to the luxury and speed of fast motor vehicles. As you might expect, since producing *Ford Cars 1945-64*, the Nostalgia Road series has now expanded to cover a diverse range of subjects, including ice cream vans and police cars.

Throughout the two decades that followed World War II, the automobile influenced our lives. It entered our fantasy lives too, a fact that almost certainly came about by the growing influence of the television screen. Interestingly, 40-years on, nearly everyone remembers the big Fords in *Z-Cars* and the lovely Emma Peel with her Lotus Elan in *The Avengers*. In the same programme, John Steed's vintage Bentley became as much a star as the actor, meanwhile the Saint's Volvo brought new devotees to the Scandinavian motor manufacturer. They were as popular in their day as Lovejoy's Morris Minor and the Jaguar MkII driven by John Thaw as *Inspector Morse* in more recent times. In fact, they were probably more popular, as they introduced a new audience to the world of private motoring. Along with the motor manufacturers' advertising of the day, the dream of car-ownership was well and truly promulgated.

The period covered by this book was not only a time of change within our lives, but a growing up and a time of expansion. It was also, sadly, sometimes a time of death within the British motor manufacturing industry as names like Alvis, Jowett, Armstrong Siddeley and a long list of great firms closed their doors for the last time. Fortunately, examples of these Marques have survived and are still to be found with caring owners.

The Ford Motor Company has, in a way, been a family of cars with what were (during the period covered by this book) often quite subtle changes from one model to another, rather than a series of radical developments. Although entering the 1930s with the assembly of mainly American-inspired models, the firm's introduction of the model 7Y (an 8hp family saloon) showed what Ford could design and build in this country! By 1937 Ford of Britain introduced the 10hp model 7W, after which Dagenham became less dependent on its American parent for its new models.

As the pictures in this chapter show, the models that Ford were producing in the 1930s had progressively developed a more stylish look, and by the outbreak of war in 1939 the British-built models were considerably less-angular in appearance than the models produced in the first three decades of this century. Attractive saloons, for both family and business use, featured in the V8 models and the 10hp Fords.

Inside a couple of years the company had moved on and both 7Y and 7W models were replaced in 1939, by the E04A and the E93A models respectively. These new cars were similarly bodied from the windscreen back, and as we will show, both these would later develop into the E494A and the E493A models of the post-war years. As for the larger cars, what then? Well after the various American-inspired V8s, like the Model 62, Model 90, and Model 91 etc., it was a time for change. This led us to the post-war V8 Pilot, and the introduction of new 'British' blood. In turn this resulted in the Consul and Zephyr of 1950, which came as part of the Ford Motor Company's aim to provide continual improvements while offering sound value for money, through a range of cars to suit all income brackets and needs. That was clearly Ford's goal, for they produced almost everything, with only a really top-flight luxury car missing from their range.

The pictures on these pages show a potted history of the cars produced by Ford for the English market, and the American influence is clearly noted. However, unlike their great rivals, Vauxhall (who were acquired by the American General Motors organisation in 1925), the American influence began to diminish. At Vauxhall it was a contrary story (see Classic Marques Vol.2 - *Vauxhall Cars 1945-'64*), as the influence of the GM brands, especially that of Chevrolet, became clearly apparent in the Luton-built cars.

In post-war Britain, Ford could have been forgiven for launching a range of American designs onto the market, as so little design development was done here after September 1939. Money was in short supply, the Austerity period was upon us, and the bulk of British motor vehicle production was being directed towards the export market. So badly did the country need overseas currency to meet its wartime debts, that the exhortation went out from government to all sectors of British industry - 'Export Or Die'. In the car market this meant that even if people could afford a new vehicle, there were not enough models available to meet the demand. Consequently the infamous waiting lists began to appear, whilst at the opposite end of the scale many cars were kept on the road for far longer than they really should have been. Even used car prices increased as a consequence of the 'supply and demand' situation, with even quite un-roadworthy vehicles fetching a 'good' price.

However, the 'export boom' did have two things in its favour, certainly as far as the major British makers were concerned. Firstly it opened up export markets in countries where American, French and German automobiles had previously dominated. Secondly it stimulated a demand in the 'middle class sector' of Britain that would continue well into the 1950s. In turn this 'middle class' market would stimulate a demand from the 'working class' market, and it was in these two areas that Ford had identified its target audience. It remains significant that, for many years thereafter, the only car that Ford did not have a contender as a 'market leader' was the 'Upper Class' or prestige sector!

By the early 1950s, Ford had begun to introduce a range of modern cars to suit all pockets, but models like the Anglia, Cortina and ultimately the Escort of the late-1960s would sweep the country by storm. This post-war range is portrayed in the following pages, covering the company's models from 1945 to 1964 and what was arguably the most successful Ford car ever built, the Cortina. The changes that were progressively introduced by Ford in these 20-years were undoubtedly a major part of the golden years of motoring.

Model 62 V8 22HP 1936

Model CX 10HP 1934

Deluxe 10HP 1937

Ford Eight 1937

THE UP-RIGHT FORDS

By 1955, the products in Ford's British range were almost of entirely modern designs and the only exception was the 103E Popular. This was a small family saloon that was specifically introduced for the 1953 Earls Court Motor Show! However, the evolution of the Popular 103E came very much from the pre-war designs of the E93A Prefect and the E04A Anglia, but it was aimed at the entry level in post-war motoring market.

It was intended as a budget-priced new car, nevertheless the economies in its production were not reflected by inferior materials, but rather an eccentric simplicity. To trace the origins of this car we need to step back to the late-1930s to look at the two aforementioned Ford saloon models of that time.

Above: *A view of the 'Final Assembly Line' at Ford's Dagenham Factory. This plant was built alongside the Thames Estuary, on what was little more than reclaimed mud-flats, but it went on to become a massive complex with large areas of associated worker's housing being developed in the surrounding countryside. The view shows EO4A Anglia models having a final quality assurance inspection before being dispatched to the dealerships.*

In 1939 Ford had launched two new models, the E93A Prefect and the E04A Anglia - the 'E' designating English manufacture. Both had side-valve engines, these being 1172cc and 933cc respectively. However, it should be pointed out that the Anglia, which incidentally was the first Ford model to carry this name, also used the larger engine on its export models.

Top Right: *The 1946 8hp E04A Anglia two-door model had a 993cc side-valve engine and a power-train coupled with a floor-mounted gear lever to a three-speed box. It was primarily designed as a family saloon and thus became the most popular Ford in the post-war era.*

Middle Right: *A 1949 example of the Anglia model, this time the two-door E494A version but again an 8hp saloon. This body style was subsequently utilised in the 103E Popular model of 1953.*

Bottom Right: *The 10hp Ford of that period was the E493A Prefect four-door saloon. It had a 1172cc engine and was a further development of the Ford Prefect E93A. This post war (1949) version of the E493A shows the modernised integral headlamps and a radiator grille inspired by the more expensive V8 Pilot.*

The Prefect model was an attractive four-door family saloon of 'Six-Light' construction, that is to say three windows along each side of the car. Its boot lid was flush with the gentle rake of the back of the car, and like most Fords of the period it was bottom hinged. At the front of the car access to the engine was gained by twisting the mascot on the alligator-type bonnet. The radiator grill of the E493A was very similar to that adorning the Ford V8 Pilot, but the headlights on the Prefect were flush-fitting in the front wings.

With private car production being cut back dramatically and no new designs put forward during the war years, the E93A and E04A were 'dated' models by 1945-6. As a result they were modified to become the 10hp E493A Prefect and the 8hp E494A Anglia between 1948 and 1953. This was a stop-gap measure until new models could be launched, but even so Ford would not entirely dispense with these tried and trusted models completely and as we will see presently, they utilised elements of the two models to make the new 'budget-price' car in time for the 1953 Motor Show.

In all 192,229 examples of the E493A Prefect were built between 1948 and 1953, and whilst its 1172cc side-valve engine came from the E93A, its origins could be traced back to the power plants in the models C and the 7W of the 1935 to 1937 period. The E493A Prefects were very similar to their older sisters, although the two models are very easily distinguished by their radiator grilles, which were of a similar shape, but totally different in their construction. The front wings were also another point of identification!

The E04A, although being similarly bodied to the E494A, had a very distinctive (rather square) bonnet and an almost vertical radiator grille. The E493A was a four-door saloon (although isolated examples of commercial two-door vehicles were to be found), whereas the E93A was offered as a two- or four-door model. Fords actually advertised these models as the Fordor and the Tudor (a simple play on words, Tudor = two-door saloon etc), in addition to the Tourer or one of the rare Drop-head coupes.

Of these models just 667 Drop-head coupes are thought to have been built, as opposed to 1,028 Tourer models, meanwhile 10,170 two-door saloons and more than 100,000 of the four-door saloon cars are recorded.

Both the E493A and the E494A were discontinued in 1953, with their replacements adopting a body style similar to that used on the Consul in 1950. However, Ford were clearly conscious of the need for an entry-level car (something cheap), and to offer this they retained elements of the E493A and the E494A for an economically-priced 10hp motorcar - the Prefect 103E.

Below: *A view of a Ford Popular, whose identity is given away by the painted wheel disks, single windscreen wiper and general de-chroming of the bodywork. This is the 103E model, built from 1953 to 1959 and sporting the same 1172cc engine as the Prefect. It was a marriage of convenience, with the E493A providing its 1172cc side-valve engine, whilst the Anglia E494A donated its two-door saloon body design in order to achieve an economy model that would provide a bargain basement entry into the market. In time the 103E obtained the nickname 'Puddle-Jumper' because of its tendency to 'skip' when driven with a bit of vigour.*

Top Right: *After the introduction of the 100E range of models, the older models became known as 'Up-right' Fords. The last of these was the 103E Popular, which was introduced in 1953 as an economy model. By keeping costs down this 'no-frills' model sold well, but drivers had to put up with inconveniences such as the single windscreen wiper fitted as standard.*

Middle Right: *By way of comparison with the Popular 103E model saloon in the above view, our photograph here shows the earlier E494A Ford Anglia on which the Popular was based.Obvious differences will be noted in the Anglia's chrome-finished bumpers with over-riders, twin scuttle mounted windscreen wipers and more chrome trim, such as that around the side air in-takes and wheel hubs.*

Bottom Right: *This really splendid photograph highlights what was once a very popular form of delivery van for the small trader. Based, as it was, on the Anglia/Popular models of the time and using the same side-valve engine, these little 5-cwt E83W vans were employed in a wide variety of roles. Lack of bumpers and the fitting of the spare wheel on the near-side door to increase load space were noticeable features.*

But fashions had changed before the 103E even got to the showroom, and it was already cosmetically obsolete as it stood among the Consuls, Zephyrs and newly introduced 100E Anglia and Prefect models. These new saloons had captured the imagination, and they looked thoroughly modern cars.

Even so, there was still an audience for a base model and this was the market that Ford was aiming for! Externally, little different from the E494A Anglia, the 103E sat on narrow pressed-steel wheels. The doors, like the Anglia, were forward-hinged and had a light swage line on the lower area that emphasised the wing line. The side-opening bonnet appeared rather high and narrow, and tapered to a fine radiator grille comprised of two tall narrow oblongs. Auxiliary grilles were fitted on each side of the bonnet sides too, with the bonnet being hinged along the centre-line, which enabled it to be opened from either side.

Small headlamps were mounted on the rather wide front wings, and semaphore indicators were utilised. A high boot protruded a short way from the back of the car with a top-hinged square number plate on the lid. This arrangement allowed the bottom-hinged boot lid to be lowered for additional luggage capacity and still show the registration plate.

Contrasting the new 103E against the old E494A, you can tell that the Anglia had employed chrome bumpers complete with over-riders and chromed wheel hubcaps; whereas the economy model had body-coloured wheel hubs and a plain bumper that was painted aluminium colour. It was basically small things like this that differentiated between the two models, but these small savings allowed Ford to sell a more economically-priced car.

THE FORD PILOT V8

It was curious that the Ford Edsel, a car that had been expected to capture the American middle market, became a tremendously embarrassing sales flop; but Ford had badly estimated the market place for this particular model in the United States. The Edsel was aimed at a customer bracket between their Mercury models and the cheaper Fords, but despite all the forward-planning, advanced publicity and excessive expenditure it failed to achieve its goal. It has often been described as the right car at the wrong time!

Like the Edsel, which should have been destined for greater things in North America, there was a similar and almost parallel story in Britain with the V8 Pilot. This was a very British motor-car, but the year of its launch (1947) was plagued by post-war steel shortages, coal supply problems and severe petrol rationing and thus not the ideal year for Ford to introduce a new large car. It was intended that the Pilot would have a new 2.5 litre engine, but there were unfavourable comments about this power unit by some of those testing the car.

Above: *What made the Ford Pilot such a good car, was the fact that it had a fine 3.6 engine throbbing away under the bonnet, even though it only had a three-speed, column-change gearbox.*

In those days of severe austerity it was difficult to spend great amounts on refining oil products, so Ford opted to give the Pilot a proven V8 engine when the main production runs began in August 1947. However, despite a grand introduction, there was not an awful lot that was new in the strictest sense of the word. The body was carried over from the 1937-1939 Model 62, although the front end was entirely re-designed. It was given a splendid radiator grille, which featured narrow vertical chrome bars and a discreet V8 Pilot badge. The front wings were also re-styled, but complemented by superb huge chrome headlamps and small sidelights. New too, were the heavy-looking, fluted chrome bumpers and over-riders.

The model 62 had ambled along by the power of a 2227cc side-valve V8 whereas the new Pilot had the 3622cc under its alligator type bonnet; this engine had first appeared in the V8 Model 18 (1932) and the subsequent Model 40 (1933).

Top Right: *One of the tasks Ford's new management undertook was to ask Briggs Motor Bodies to construct a few pre-production prototypes of the Pilot as a feasibility study before Ford committed itself to commencing full production. These prototypes performed well, and shortly afterwards full production of the chassis was started at Dagenham. Briggs continued to play their part, as they fitted bodies to the chassis at their nearby works.*

Middle Right: *This is how the Ford V8 Pilot chassis looked when it was built between 1947 and 1951, and before bodywork was added by Briggs Motorbodies across the road from the Dagenham plant. Although this vehicle had a V8 engine, this was still a side-valve design and had a column-shift gear lever.*

Bottom Right: *In 1948 Ford decided to use the chassis of the Pilot for commercial applications, and it offered the E71C to be bodied by outside contractors. Vans and pick-up trucks were built on this chassis, and it could even be purchased as a very practical and attractive all-steel or 'woody' estate car (seen here). The E71C still left Dagenham as a chassis-cab, but they were developed in various styles and applications by a number of coach-builders; at least five were bodied as limousines.*

The engine had a cylinder bore of 77.79mm and a piston stroke of 95.25mm its maximum power was 85 brake horse power at 3,500 revolutions per minute, producing a top speed of around 87mph. Quite remarkable for an engine that was designed in the early 1930s, and it was certainly no slouch then even if the 0-60mph time of 20+ seconds seems a little laboured today, This came at a cost though, as a Pilot owner could expect to average around a miserly 18-20 miles per gallon in fuel, which must have caused more than a little concern with petrol being rationed as it was, when the model first put in its appearance back in those uncertain post-war days of 1947.

Internally, the new Pilot had a quality feel about it and this was clearly needed as its competition was the Wolseley 6/80, Morris Six series MS, Phase I Standard Vanguard and the like. The Pilot had fully-fitted carpets, a heater, a clock, cigarette lighter and provision for an optional radio. Comprehensive instrumentation was set in a large 'Bakelite' dashboard, but the export models had an aluminium dashboard as the Bakelite ones suffered in hot climates. Export models had vertical louvres in their bonnet side-panels too. Also on the list of fine things that the Pilot was equipped with were foot-rests for the rear seat passengers.

The bench seats, almost as comfortable as a living room sofa, were usually cloth-trimmed but leather was offered as an optional extra. For ease of maintenance, it also had a novel 'Jackall' system, which was a hydraulic jack device that operated on all four wheels. The basic price of the car was £585, but with purchase tax this went up to a staggering £748 5s, and if you wanted a model with leather trim it would cost a princely £764 4s 5d.

As mentioned earlier, this commercial version was also developed into several types of attractive estate car, either panelled in steel or as a 'woody', which was often referred to at that time as a shooting brake. Perhaps the most famous shooting brake was one that carried the registration mark VUL 3. It was built in 1951 with a chassis some 12-inches longer than the standard and was taller too. Designed especially for King George VI, it was unique in having a floor gear-change as His Majesty did not care for a column change. The steel-work was painted a dignified green and the radiator and bumpers were black. It spent much of its time on the Royal Estates at Balmoral and Sandringham where it still remains today.

For normal customers, when a 'woody' Pilot was ordered from a Ford dealership it was usually fitted with a body built by the firm of Garners of Acton, West London who (incidentally) built the body on the King's car. Yet, several other companies bodied Pilots too! The Royal patronage was however, a valuable sales asset.

Ford dealers, W.H.Perry of North Finchley made eight Woody's for example and W.J. Reynolds finished several chassis cabs as pick-up trucks. Production of the saloon version came to an end in May 1951 after 22,155 examples had been built, but a few of the E71C models were continued into 1952 and when production stopped, 3,807 of these chassis units had been made. There had been plans for a new 14hp Pilot but, despite some development and planning, this idea was cancelled with the success of the new Consul and Zephyr models that had appeared at the Earls Court show in 1950.

Below: *Here we see the Ford Pilot as introduced in 1947. It was based on the body shell of the V8-62 model, however it was completely re-designed from the scuttle forward. Originally it was intended that the Pilot would be powered by a recently developed 2.5 litre engine, but in the event it was decided to use the tried and tested 85hp/3,622cc version of the V8.*

CONSUL, ZEPHYR, ZODIAC MkI

As the 1950s began, Ford progressed with its desire to have a range of cars to suit all income brackets from the Popular 103E, through the 100E Anglia and Prefect range to the larger Consul, Zephyr Six and Zephyr-Zodiac. Two of these larger cars had been introduced in October 1950 (the four-cylinder Consul with its 1508cc over-head valve engine and the 2262cc six-cylinder ohv Zephyr Six) in time for exhibition at Earls Court, but it was not until New Year's Day 1951 that production really started. When the range was introduced Ford used the 'Three Box Design' (bonnet, cabin and boot) for the first time in Britain, as prior to this all the earlier models had separate wings. These larger Fords with their full width body shells also had other innovations, as these were of monocoque construction and this offered useful weight savings over the earlier products that had used a separate chassis.

Above: *One of the new breed of Ford family saloons was the Mark I Consul, designed for the 1950s with a 1508 cc over-head valve engine. The car seen here is Ford demonstrator UPU 418 and possibly pictured in the Cotswolds.*

Interestingly, these were the first British cars to employ the Macpherson Strut suspension system; this was a radical change from previous Ford engineering policy and, though it was so revolutionary at the time, its effective simplicity has since made it a widely copied concept. Ford's bolt on panel policy was also clearly evident, with front wings, front panels and the lower half of the rear wing being produced in this fashion; the upper section of the rear wings however, along with the boot sill formed an integral part of the body. The Consul and Zephyr Six were identical from the windscreen to the rear of the car, but the Zephyr Six employed a longer front section to house the in-line six-cylinder engine.

Top Left: *An official view of a Mark 1 Consul, a model built between 1950 and 1956, and one that changed the styling of British motoring fashion. Along with its brethren in Ford's large car range, it also did much to introduce thousands of Britons to the joys of 'modern' travel.*

Middle Left: *Two MkI Consuls, both of which are later examples of the model as shown by the rear light construction. The picture also illustrates the difference in the registration plate lamp housing; those on the Consul being body coloured but chrome-plated on the Zephyr models.* Robert W Berry

Bottom Left: *The Consul convertible model was produced by Carbodies of Coventry with the official sanction of Dagenham. Pictured here with a closed hood, the two-door example retains its rounded appearance, but with the hood lowered the Consul had a definite American flare and yet was a uniquely British car.*

Both of the new models had headlights built high into the leading curved corners of the front wings, with sidelights below, but one of the main features that differentiated between the models was the radiator grille. As will be seen from the pictures on the left, the Consul's grille was a regular oblong of convex vertical slats with a chrome finish; the central bar being much wider to carry the Ford badge. The bumpers were also a little different, as the Consul normally featured plain bumpers whilst the Zephyr Six wore over-riders. Both models used the same plain chromed wheel trims with a slightly-raised circular centre section.

During their production years, some of the six-cylinder cars enjoyed various successful rallying careers, as would the MkII models that would eventually succeed them in 1956. The Consul also enjoyed a little of the limelight on the race and rally circuits, but they were obviously over-shadowed by the greater potential of the bigger cars. The success of these models actually encouraged Ford of Great Britain to set up its own motor-sport competition department in 1952.

Ford duly prepared four Zephyr Six saloon cars for the 1953 Monte Carlo Rally, which was actually won by a Dutchman named Maurice Gatsonides in a beige Zephyr saloon registered VHK 194. Other successes followed in both works and privately-entered Zephyr cars, for example Nancy Mitchell won the ladies cup on the 1953 Lisbon rally and the 1954 RAC Rally was won by Edward and Cuthbert Harrison! Yet it was the production car market that really interested the Ford Motor Company, and in October 1953 the Dagenham plant turned out the first top of the range model in the Consul-Zephyr family.

This was the comprehensively equipped, 'Zephyr-Zodiac', which was one of the most glamorous British saloon cars of its time. The new large Fords had caused quite a sensation on their introduction in 1950 with their slab sided, trans-Atlantic styling and spacious appearance.

The introduction of this 'flagship' in the Ford range went even further. With its exciting appearance it was, for many, to be the dawning of a new exciting motoring era. The model had a very great impact on the British public and indeed the British motor industry as a whole! Internally, Ford continued the glamourous styling effect with two-tone leather upholstery and re-styled door trims with the lower sections carpeted to match the floors. There was a vanity mirror on the passenger sun-visor, an electric clock, a cigarette lighter and new head-linings in woollen textile. Even so it was the external appearance that had the greatest effect.

Both six-cylinder cars had their rear badges on either side of the chromed number-plate lamp housing on the boot, but the four-cylinder model had the word Consul in chrome fitted on the registration plate lamp housing. The final touches to the Zephyr-Zodiac were a new bonnet mascot, styled rather like a futuristic aeroplane and, most noticeable of all a set of beautiful white-walled tyres.

Top Right: *Seen at a vehicle rally in 1985, we find a rare survivor of the MkI estate conversions, which were available from 1954 onwards on both the Consul (pictured) and the Zephyr Six models. This was achieved by Abbott's of Farnham, who cut across the roof above the rear window and down the rear roof pillars (a short distance back from the door frames) and along the top of the rear wings. They then welded a new section in its place to comprise the estate 'body', and this was duly fitted with windows that harmonised with the rear passenger doors that had been retained. A new single-piece door (which was hinged at the off-side) was produced for the rear of the estate and this used the original rear screen from the saloon.* Robert W Berry

Middle Right: *With the introduction of the EOTA Consul and the EOTTA Zephyr models, Ford became one of the leaders of a new, bright motoring look in the 1950s. Variations of the basic saloon models followed quickly, with Abbott of Farnham producing estate cars and Carbodies of Coventry creating convertibles. Our view here shows one of the Consul convertible models with the hood in the raised position and shows to good effect the really excellent standard achieved.*

Bottom Right: *After the saloon cars had become firmly established, Ford and the specialist bodywork company 'Carbodies' of Coventry turned their attention to a convertible model. After extensive development, two-door convertible versions of the Consul and the Zephyr Six became available, although for some strange reason the Zephyr-Zodiac was not later offered in this form. The Zephyr Six had a hood that was raised electrically to the De-ville position, but it could be ordered with a manually raised hood if you wanted to save £45. Conversely, the Consul had a manually raised hood, although an optional power hood was available at extra cost.*

Top Left: *The Ford Zephyr-Zodiac was, as the name suggests, an up-market model of the six-cylinder car. These models were usually finished in one of the many two-tone colour schemes, as the example illustrated here, but sharing the same body and being mechanically similar to the Zephyr Six. The badging of the two six-cylinder EOTTA cars was a distinctive feature. Whereas the Zephyr had a chrome-plated 'Zephyr Six' cast script on the leading edge of its bonnet the new luxury model had its Zephyr-Zodiac gold-plated.*

Middle Left: *The reader will observe from this close-up view and the one above that, whilst the script on the Zephyr and Zodiac models was separated by the radiator recess, the Zodiac's was mounted higher. This was to avoid being obscured by the fog and spot lamps that were mounted as standard on the bumper over-riders. Seen while awaiting restoration near Dewsbury in 1992, this particular car (which was originally owned by the theatrical impresarios, the Grade brothers) has now been restored to pristine condition by its dedicated owner Colin Moorhouse.*

Bottom Left *This profile view of a Zephyr Six saloon, clearly illustrates the difference in the length of the bodywork between the four- and six-cylinder models forward of the windscreen. This car is clearly one of the pre-1953 models built and would have caused quite a stir with its trans-Atlantic styling, which featured enclosed wings. Added to this was the innovation of new OHV engines and the MacPherson-strut independent front suspension.*

This successful recipe of Ford's styling, engineering par-excellence and overall value for money was such, that during the entire production programme of the MkI models (1950-1956), there were only the most nominal changes. One of these came in the autumn of 1951, following a criticism of the lack of internal stowage space, which in turn led to the dashboard and instrument housing being redesigned,

Yet, whilst this new dashboard was fitted to the models featured at the Earls Court motor show in 1951, it was not until the following September that it was put into production models. The speedometer, fuel gauge and ammeter had previously been in an elongated clover-leaf styled housing, whilst on the passenger side the same design had been used for a glove-box. However, with the new variant it was deleted in favour of a wide parcel shelf below a new curved dashboard; earlier cars becoming nicknamed the 'Flat-dash', among old Ford enthusiasts.

From their introduction until the Autumn of 1953, the original cars had used the semaphore type of traffic indicator, but after this date all models had flashing lights, white at the front (within the sidelight unit) and red at the rear (though these were later changed to amber lenses). As a matter of fact, the entire rear lamp unit (except the indicators) were re-designed the following year, as part of Ford's policy of continual improvement.

The rarest version of the Consul and Zephyr range was designed and built at Ford's Geelong plant Australia. To suit the needs of the vast open spaces of that continent, the enterprising staff at the Ford plant came up with the idea of a pick-up truck or 'utility` as they called them 'Down Under'. Unfortunately Dagenham did not have the same enthusiasm and the production reached double figures, but only just: a mere 11 were made before the project was ended!

The last of the Ford Consul, Zephyr Six, Zephyr-Zodiac cars, came off the assembly line at Dagenham, on 22nd February 1956, the MkII models having gone into production the previous day. Yet, during the production years of the MkI models, 231,481 examples of the four-cylinder Consul (EOTA) vehicles were built. With a further total of 175,311 six-cylinder (EOTTA) models being made, of which 22,634 were the luxury Zephyr-Zodiac.

Below: *The MkI Ford Zephyr-Zodiac range was built between 1953 and 1956 and invariably tended to feature a two-tone paint scheme, which was further highlighted by the wide white wall tyres (as shown in this illustration). As a matter of interest, we might add that although single tone colours were available, (Black often being the usual choice), the majority of Zephyr-Zodiac's were painted in the two-tone scheme. The colours were separated at the waist swage line, where a full-length chrome strip was located; a feature that also appeared on the Consul and Zephyr around this time. At the front of the Zephyr-Zodiac, the colours were divided at the point where the bonnet and radiator grille met, whilst they were divided at the rear where the boot lid met the sill. These divisions were at the same height as the side swage line thus giving the colour division, perfect harmony!*

THE 100E SERIES

Whilst we have so far discussed the larger car market Ford enjoyed in the early 1950s, the growing need for a moderately-priced family saloon car was also becoming increasingly evident in this period. In response to this market trend, Ford introduced its economical 100E range of small cars that embodied modern methods of construction.

Because they were built along the same principles as the Consul and Zephyr models, the body styling was in many ways rather similar although the dimensions were more compact. A standard body shape was employed for two fairly similarly 100E series cars in 1953, these being the four-door Prefect and the two-door Anglia. The overall dimensions were identical, with a total length of 12' 7¼" on a 7' 3" wheelbase: the height was 4' 9" and it was 5' 0½" wide. Yet, these compact dimensions were neatly disguised by the attractive body styling.

Above: *Similar in styling to the MkI Consul, Zephyr, Zodiac range, the smaller 100E series (illustrated by the Anglia model pictured above) was an instant 'hit' with drivers who wanted modern styling and a lower price.*

Both 100E models were of conventional front engine-rear wheel drive layout, with a side-valve engine. This was a four cylinder 1172cc unit, with a bore and stroke of 63.5mm x 92.5mm. These models were all driven through a gearbox with three forward and one reverse gear, which had a floor-mounted gear lever. Only body styling differentiated the various types, for instance the Anglia was furnished with a radiator grille of three slightly curved steel bars, finished in aluminium paint; whilst, on the other hand, the Prefect's grille was constructed from thin vertical slats in the same general oblong shape, but it had a gentle convex from top to bottom. Both models had a forward hinged bonnet, with the respective name on the leading edge.

Top Right: *The 100E model Prefect, a four-door saloon with a distinctive grille of vertical slats and chrome headlight surrounds. Its styling and origins can easily be demonstrated by turning back to look once again at the earlier pictures of MkI Ford Consul and Zephyr models.*

Middle Right: *Aimed squarely at the car buyer who wanted crisp modern looks in their new car but with more economical operating costs, Ford offered their new 100E range. These new models superseded the E493A Prefect and the E494A Anglia in 1953. The two new models shared the same basic body style, which echoed the styling of the larger models that had been introduced in 1950*

Bottom Right: *When the 105E Anglia was launched in 1959, the obsolete 100E Anglia body shell was used to create the entry level Ford Popular 100E. This was a marketing strategy that had been used earlier in the decade with the 103E.*

Headlamps were set in the top of the wings, with a rectangular sidelight/indicator below. On the Prefect the lamp bezels were finished in chrome plate, but on the Anglia they were painted in the body colour. Similarly the Prefect had chromed bumpers, whereas aluminium paint was employed on the earlier Anglia model. The wheel arches had a slight lip around them, whilst the rear ones were noticeably lower and this tended to lengthen the style of the body in an appealing way. Finally, the 100E models had plain, chromed wheel discs with a central pimple, very similar to those on their larger brethren the Consul/Zephyrs.

Improvements to the range came first in 1955 with the introduction of a deluxe model, followed by styling changes to the standard models in 1957. Larger rear-light clusters were introduced, and all models were then provided with a bigger rear window to improve visibility. The Prefect lost its winged bonnet mascot, which was replaced with the smooth, swept 'V' ornament that thereafter adorned all the 100E models. Deluxe models had a thin chrome-plated strip along the waist swage line, and chrome inserts to the headlamp bezels.

On 23rd September 1955 the Squire Deluxe was announced as the two-door estate version of the Prefect saloon, which featured the same appointments. For the first two years of its life, the model featured a little wood trim along its flanks - perhaps copying the American 'station-wagon' vogue.

For the more economy-minded, Ford introduced the Escort Estate a few days after the Squire; this being a less well-equipped estate version based on the Anglia. The Escort had the same three bar radiator grille as the Anglia, but from 1957 onwards both models featured a re-designed lightweight grille constructed of horizontal and vertical cross-mesh. On the standard models this was finished in aluminium paint, though the deluxe model was given the luxury of a chrome finish.

Top Left: *A model 100E Popular Deluxe, two-door saloon, showing the circular tail lights unique to this model. This actual car was registered in Dewsbury, West Yorkshire, and is photographed in the nearby town of Mirfield.* Robert Berry

Middle Left: *During 1957 the Anglia models were modernised with an increase in size of the rear windscreen, and a new style of radiator grille (compare with the lower view), these features were carried over to the 100E Popular model.*

Bottom Left: *In this superb official photograph we see a young lady delighted with her early Deluxe Anglia 100E. Notice how the slight camber of the front and rear profiles, the full length chrome strip and the rear wheel arch (being slightly lower than that of the front) all help to give a look of motion.*

The production of the Squire Deluxe came to an end in 1959, whilst at the same time the 100E Prefect was phased out. A replacement for the 100E Prefect was found in the 107E Prefect, which (although bodily identical) had a number of major differences from the earlier model. The most significant was the use of the new overhead valve engine and drive train that had been developed for the new 105E (rake-back window) Anglia.

With the development of the new Anglia and Classic models, with their controversial backward sloping rear windows, the end of the 100E range was signalled. The Anglia 100E was replaced by the Anglia 105E in September 1959, and in a sense this paved the way for the Popular 100E. Following their success with the economical 103E in 1953, Ford once more employed the concept of using a superseded model to produce a budget-priced family car. Although we may now be chronologically jumping the gun somewhat, it might be logical to discuss what happened to the 100E body shell when it was superseded by its successor Ford Anglia 105E in 1959.

The result was basically a de-trimmed Anglia with the cross-meshed grille of 1957 vintage, however the tail lights were different items - being separate circular units with a round reflector above in a vertical plane. The 100E Popular was available in standard or deluxe versions, but the standard model was very basic, lacking such items as door pulls, interior lights, passenger sun visor, opening quarter lights and ash trays - all of which featured on the deluxe version. The Escort estate remained available until 1961, whilst the 100E Popular stayed in production until the summer of 1962, when the era of the small side-valve Fords came to its final end but the body shape went on to house the OHV engine in the 107E model.

Ford's marketing department were not quite satisfied, because the body shape of the Anglia did not lend itself to a four-door configuration. Sadly sales of competitively priced four-door saloons such as the Morris 1000 and the like were taking business away from Ford to BMC; Triumph actually had a similar problem with its two-door Herald, but Ford felt something had to be done.

Before looking in further detail at the 107E, we should mention the commercial development of the 100E, although this will be more fully considered in a future book, *Ford Light Commercials Of The 1950s & '60s*. Today, car-derived vans are quite common creations, but the arrival of a commercial derivative of the 100E series was quite a big step for Ford at that time. Prior to this it had produced a separate range of commercial vehicles based on chassis, chassis-cab and factory-bodied vans,

The most successful of these was arguably the Ford E83W, which had been introduced in March 1938. This 10-cwt semi forward-control truck was powered by a 10hp four-cylinder engine and cost £168 in basic van guise. There was also an option to purchase it in the chassis or chassis-cab versions, and a wide variety of body applications were fitted. Yet it was clearly a dated design by the time hostilities ended in 1945. Nevertheless the E83W soldiered on until September 1957, and by the time production ended over 188,000 had been built at Dagenham,

Although the E83W model (see page 11) had received a few small improvements during its long life, there was no way that it could compete with BMC with their highly successful Morris Minor light commercials for performance or indeed with Bedford with carrying capacity. Ford did have plans for a vehicle for the 10- to 12-cwt market, but what they were concerned with at the moment was the 5- to 7-cwt range

Whilst the E83W had proved to be a useful post-war commercial, Ford had identified an emerging market for a lighter commercial vehicle in the 5 to 7-cwt range. Accordingly, in July 1954, Ford expanded the 100E range with the introduction of the 300E. This initially provided a 5-cwt van that had the Anglia's front end styling, but it was followed a year later by a 7-cwt van that employed the Prefect radiator grille. Unlike the estate cars with their split-tailgate, these van versions had conventional doors featuring a small window in each. These vans were to prove such a successful contribution to the world of compact commercial vehicles that with the introduction of the succeeding models the range of commercials in this class was continued.

Top Right: *This picture illustrates the early Escort estate, which used the same slatted radiator grille as the Anglia. Then, with the styling revision of 1957, the Anglia and Escort estate models received the new style of radiator grille given to the saloon.*

Middle Right: *The Squire Deluxe estate is seen with the earlier wooden trim on its side. Again, a 1957 styling change resulted in this feature being changed, although this type of radiator grille was retained*

Bottom Right: *The van bodied version of the 100E was more correctly known as 300E series, and the working example seen here is a Sheffield registered 7-cwt Thames.*

FORD PREFECT 107E

The advent of the new 107E economy model filled at least two gaps in the Ford range; namely cheapness and versatility. For instance,after the arrival of the two-door Anglia (105E/123E) models, anyone who wanted a four-door Ford had to make quite a climb up the financial ladder to achieve the level of the Ford Consul. More importantly, not everyone wanted a car of the Consul's dimensions or that size of engine.

The interim solution was to up-rate the 100E Prefect body-shell with the new engine, running gear and gear-box of the 105E Anglia. In short, Ford had come up with a winner again, providing a new budget-price four-door saloon car without further development costs and the associated teething problems that all new cars face. The new Prefect with its four-speed gearbox became a firm family favourite. Fuel consumption was also improved, with an average of around 35 mph as opposed to something like 30mph in the 100E. The body was still the same, with enough accommodation for four adults, though it would take five at a pinch.

Above: *The 107E was not the most luxurious car for the 'Swinging Sixties', but for the economy-minded motorist, or those wanting to upgrade from a motor-cycle or public transport it was just 'Fab'.* Robert Berry

The 107E differed very little from the 100E, but it featured the larger rear screen and new rear lamp units of the later 100E Prefect. It also had the same frontal treatment, but to give it a more elegant feel the 107E was finished in two-tone colours, which were separated at the waist swage line by a full-length chrome strip.

However, before reaching the front light unit, this piece of body trim came back on a 'dog-leg' to the front wheel-arch, giving a forward thrust to the lower colour. The 107E Ford Prefect was manufactured from October 1959 and deleted from the Ford range in March 1961, after 38,154 examples had been produced. Its natural successor was the Classic and later still the fabulous four-door Cortina, which epitomised Ford's most successful entry into the medium-priced family and commercial-traveller's car market.

Above: *In the tradition of the founder of the company, to bring motoring to the masses, Ford re-introduced their E494A Anglia in a de-trimmed form as an economy entry level car in 1953. This model was known as the Popular 103E and was easily distinguished from its ancestor by the painted hub-caps, plain bumpers, lack of chrome trim and single windscreen wiper, This model, although essentially of pre-war design, was to remain in production until 1959.*

Right: *Sharing the same body as the Mk.I Zephyr Six, the Ford Zephyr-Zodiac was one of the most flamboyant British motor cars when introduced by Ford in 1953. Without doubt the new styling owed a lot to the post-war American influence, particularly in its almost standard option of duo-tone paintwork,and white-wall tyres. It did by way of its engineering merits though, appeal to a great deal of customers.*

Above: *Ford's top of the range model during the period 1956 to 1962 was the Zodiac 206E model, an example of which is seen with the superbly finished car illustrated here. Beneath that large, stylish bonnet was a wonderful 2553cc six-cylinder OHV engine, coupled to a transmission with a three-speed column gear-change, although an optional automatic version was available.*

Left: *As an alternative to the two- and-four door saloon car versions of the Ford Prefect and Anglia 100E models (aimed at the small family car buyer), Ford also offered a series of estate cars. However, rather than being conversions of the saloon cars, these rather versatile models were actually based on the 300E vans. Two estate models were offered, these being the Escort and the Squire Deluxe, which was the more up-market model. Illustrated here is a pre-1957 example of the Squire, for after this year the wooden side-trim was discontinued.*

Above: *The Ford Consul Classic was often the subject of some controversy, but as this official view shows it was without doubt a fashionable and stylish car. The body had a low radiator grill, that was partially hidden by the plain bumper, and a swage line that ended in subtle fins over the rear light clusters. Whilst the rake and wide sweep of the windscreen all helped to enhance a styling that suggested motion even when the car was stationary, thus aping an American styling trend of the time.*

Right: *Ford's Anglia 105E and 123E models were among the most popular compact cars of the early 1960s. Powered by either 997cc or 1198cc OHV four-cylinder engines, the Anglia had a traditional rear wheel drive layout via a new four-speed gearbox. With a purchase price of £589 for the 105E model when launched in 1959. Ford managed to sell 1,083,960 models to an eager general public, as well as the race and rally enthusiasts.*

Above: *Ford's faith in their new Cortina was so complete that within a short period of its launch, the Lotus version was announced. This was based on the two-door body shell and used the same 1,558cc Lotus-Ford twin-cam engine, and close-ratio gearbox that was fitted to the Lotus Elan, (a lightweight Glass-fibre bodied sports car that had been introduced in October 1962). Our photograph here shows the unusual red and gold livery as most of the production models were in the white with a green flash colour scheme.*

Left: *Although Ford had introduced their new Zephyr and Zodiac models in the spring of 1962, it was not until October of that year that Fords traditional estate car conversion specialist, Abbott of Farnham, exhibited an Estate version of these new models and as can be clearly seen from this splendid view this looked like a planned creation rather than a conversion of a saloon.*

CONSUL, ZEPHYR, ZODIAC MkII

As the decade progressed, Ford's large car range was completely re-designed in 1956 and shown to the public in February of that year. The MkII Consul, Zephyr and Zodiac models were bigger and better than the earlier models, which thereafter became retrospectively known as the MkIs. Not only were they bigger in almost every dimension, but they were also better in many ways. For a start, Ford re-designed a good many of the component parts, improved the braking systems and gave a better weight distribution.

Yet it was at the heart of the car, the engine, where some of the most significant mechanical changes were made. Although the four-cylinder Consul shared the same bore dimension as the six-cylinder Zephyr-Zodiac cars, these were increased to 82.55mm x 79.5mm. In turn this increased the swept volumes to 1703cc on the Consul and 2553cc on the other two models.

Above: *Attractive, fashionable young ladies were often used in the official photographs of most new cars of that time, as for example this 1956 MkII Zodiac saloon. The absence of chrome trim from the rear roof pillar and the car's circular sidelights betray its age.*

A two-door convertible quickly followed the saloon car into production, and towards the end of 1956 an estate version was once again offered by E.D. Abbott of Farnham. In many ways this was identical to the conversion on the MkI estate models, but there were a number of subtle differences, not least of which was seen on the window-line.

Meanwhile the new saloon cars followed the same basic design principles of the MkI models, but they had a completely fresh style with an up to the minute trans-Atlantic flair. They also had an air of beauty and grace, and as modern-day advertisers might say, 'more than a little panache'.

Top Left: *Robert Berry found this 1956 Consul inside a barn in West Yorkshire, from where he rescued it several years ago. It was then restored by Colin Moorhouse, before being pictured outside Robert's home near Penrith.*

Middle Left: *Although this was the standard colour split for the estate cars produced by Abbott when finished in a two-tone scheme, Zodiac models like this were also available in a sandwich effect scheme where the bodywork below the straight waistline would be the same colour as that on the upper bodywork.*

Bottom Left: *Here is a truly beautiful example of a 'Honeycomb' grill pre-1958 Zephyr convertible, the ivory paintwork admirably contrasting with the red hood*

The bodywork on all three models was almost identical from the windscreen backwards. On the Consul there was a subtle curve to the top corner of the rear wings, on which Ford mounted the rear light units - these were a triangular amber indicator at the top, a rectangular rear light in the centre and a small round reflector below. This arrangement differed from the Zephyr-Zodiac models that had an identical rear wing, but had a more squared-off style, though each model again had different light clusters. Furthermore the Zodiac, in its MkII form, was a different model in its own right. It also had a ribbed metal trim on the rear panel below the boot lid that embraced the rear wings just below the rear lights. Rear registration plates were hinged and sprung at the bottom, allowing access to the fuel filler cap.

All three models had bolt-on front wings, though as before there was a difference in the length between the four-cylinder and six-cylinder cars, but on the MkII models, the whole of the rear wings became part of the body structure. The front panel below the radiator grille was still made as a bolt-on item and the bonnet and boot were counter-balanced. However, it was the panoramic views afforded by the new body styling that figured as the major feature on the MkIIs. From the driver's seat, the forward view was excellent, with the bonnet sweeping gracefully down between the wings. The style of these wings had the added advantage of making manoeuvring the car accurate and almost effortless, even in the most confined spaces. The rear-screen had the same panoramic features, with the pillars set back so as not to impede the driver's field of vision. The rear view took in both of the rear wings, and because of this, even the task of reversing these large cars was an easy exercise.

The major identifying feature of each model was the radiator grille, with all three models being different. On the Consul it was a wide oblong with a mesh-effect, the top of which had a gentle curve from end to end with a separate trim section that followed the curve. The Consuls also had a chrome-plated trim item, in the form of a narrow casting which swept round the bottom corners of the wing just above the bumper.

The radiator grilles on the Zephyr and Zodiac were of a similar fashion to those carried on the MkI models, but were wider and more streamlined. Conversely, the Zodiac grille was formed of thin horizontal bars, with a small casting of fine vertical bars above the central section. Zephyr grilles were a one-piece structure of the same overall shape but constructed in an elongated waffle shape, although this was re-designed in October 1957.

The MkII Zodiacs were often finished in a two-tone colour scheme separated at the chrome waist band, giving an imposing impression especially when shod with white-wall tyres, as we can see from page 26 of this book. Originally there was a choice of five two-tone paint schemes or black for the Zodiac, (the example illustrated on page 26 being black and red), and eight monotone colour schemes for the Consul and Zephyr models. These were Black, Sarum Blue, Carlisle Blue, Wells Fawn, Ivory, Warwick Green, Corfe Grey and Hereford Green. Interiors were also usually two-tone, for example a black car might have a red/cream interior and early cars had buttoned vinyl seats. In the autumn of 1957 Ford continued its expansion into the quality car market when the Consul Deluxe was introduced, with interior appointments almost to the specification of the Zodiac models. Externally the deluxe models were distinguished by a second colour applied to the roof panel and by their chrome-plated rear lamp clusters.

Following the introduction of this model, the paint colours were revised so that early in 1958 you could have, Kenilworth Blue with a black roof, or Pembroke Coral with a Dover White roof, alternatively there was a Dover White body with a Ludlow Green roof, whilst Pembroke Coral also appeared as a roof colour on Durham Beige coloured cars. Though this continual revision of colour schemes was an on-going process, it was apparent someone at Ford had a fondness for place names.

Top Right: *Moving now to the second production phase of the MkII, we look at what were known as the 'Lowline' models. However this Consul variant of the MkII is somewhat a hybrid model as it employs rear wings of a 'Highline' and a 'Lowline' roof panel and lamp bezels - dating this as an early 1959 production.*

Middle Right: *A 'Lowline' Zephyr 206E saloon model pictured at the rear of Beaumont Brothers Garage, Meltham, West Yorkshire in the company of a Morris Minor 1000 convertible.* Alan Earnshaw

Bottom Right: *This photograph graphically illustrates the main difference between the very small amount of Dagenham built Mk.II based pick-up trucks and those manufactured at Fords plant in Australia. This British built example of a Zephyr really raises the question of why a far greater number of these utility vehicles were not built.*

Top Left: *In this sequence of pictures we show the MkII range of convertibles, all of which were produced from standard Ford saloons modified by Messrs. Carbodies of Coventry. The first view is of an early Consul model*

Middle Left: *Carbodies' products featured regularly at the Earls Court Motor show, and due to their stylish and sporty look they achieved a significant number of sales amongst the discerning motorists. For many others they were, as this Zephyr clearly illustrates as much a fashion statement as are the cabriolet cars of today.*

Bottom Left: *Even down to today these cars have a remarkable pulling power, and some Ford dealers still have them in their showrooms to attract the public to more modern cars. One such dealer is the firm of Beaumont Brothers, whose garage was built on the site of the stables once owned by the Earnshaw family haulage and carting business at Meltham in West Yorkshire.*

In February 1959, three years after introduction, a modernisation programme was carried out to take the range into the 1960s. All models were given a lower, flatter roof panel and chrome-plated headlamp bezels. The thin chrome-plate waist strip now ran all the way to the end of the rear wings, whereas before it had stopped short on the Consul and curved upward on the Zephyr. The Consul's rear wings were then squared up, and the deluxe version had chrome-plated strips added to the four horizontal ribs of the back panel.

All three models received new rear light clusters and wider, brighter window trims. The interior was re-designed with a padded fascia and a lower instrument cowl replaced the semi-circular type in earlier models. Newer, brighter colours were introduced, and the estate cars were still available in either a two-tone or monotone finish. The colour division (depending on a new chrome body-strip that curved down from near the front windscreen) then ran parallel with the waist strip to the end of the vehicle. Zodiac estates were also available in a two-tone scheme in a sandwich effect, in addition to the standard two-tone and monotone schemes. All modernised MkII cars were referred to as 'Lowline' models whereas the pre-1959 cars became known as 'Highline' models.

In 1960 all three models became available with front disc brakes as an optional extra, as opposed to the standard drum brakes operating on all four wheels; but the following year disc brakes themselves became standard. Also in 1961, the Consul was re-named the Consul 375 to differentiate it from the new Consul Classic. The Consul 375 logo then appeared in chrome lettering on the right-hand corner of the boot lid and in the radiator badge. In the spring of 1962 the Consul, Zephyr, Zodiac models were deleted from the Ford range, with the MkII models having been produced for six years and two months.

Besides the saloons, convertibles and estate cars, the Dagenham plant also manufactured a handful of pick-up trucks. However these differed greatly from the pick-ups and estates manufactured at the Australian factory that were aimed at the peculiar Austral-Asian 'utility' market. A good many of the British pick-ups found employment with small businessmen, but because of their power they became exceptionally popular with both builders and small farmers who used them for milk deliveries.

The MkII saloons were very popular with a large number of police forces, both home and abroad, whilst they were also held in high esteem by a number of rally drivers. Though in the main it was the private motorist who ensured the success of the range introduced as the 'Three Graces' when they were introduced in 1956 - a description in which they excelled.

Yet, despite the fact that the re-vamp in 1959 was designed to prolong the Consul, Zephyr, Zodiac range into the 1960s, Ford really wanted a range of cars that was more in tune with what people were expecting in the 1960s. At the end of the 1950s, they had made considerable progress in this regard, as the 100E series was to be succeeded by the new Anglia 105E in 1959. However, this left a rather sizeable gap between the two-door 997cc engine Anglia 105E and the Consul four-door saloon with its 1703cc engine. As we will later see, this gap was to be filled by an entirely new model, the Ford Consul Classic, which was sold in either two- or four-door saloon guise.

With these projects under way, attention could be given to an up-date of the bigger cars. Although the MkI and MkII Ford Zodiacs had brightened the motoring scene enormously when they appeared in their vivacious party mood in the 1950s, Ford wanted to move the models more up-market. Accordingly, Ford were already setting out the design for the MkIII version, which would succeed them in 1962; a design in which radical changes were to become evident.

Top Right: *Viewed in this picture, we see a restored MkII 'Lowline' Consul Estate, painted in Pompadour Blue and Chateau Grey, and looking as glamorous in the 1980s as it did when built 25 years earlier.* Robert Berry

Middle Right: *A 'Highline' Zephyr estate which dates from around 1958 as prior to this date Zephyr models had a honeycomb style radiator grille and from 1959 the 'Lowline' models made their appearance.* Robert Berry Collection

Bottom Right: *A 'Lowline' Zodiac estate is seen in Bradford in the late 1980s, where a poster advertising the new Ford Sierra, (seen in the background) makes an interesting contrast. Little wonder that, when the first edition of this book went to press in 1997, Ford could rightly be celebrating being the nation's favourite car manufacturer for 21 years.* Robert Berry

THE ANGLIA 105E/123E

By the latter part of the 1950s Ford were once again in desperate need of a new car with modern styling to meet the needs of the small car market in the 1960s. At that time most of the offerings from British car manufacturers were along the same lines, with round bulbous features. The Morris 1000, Austin A35, Hillman Minx and Ford's own 100E range all fell into the same concept, and much the same was evidenced in the European market, with perhaps the bubble-shaped Volkswagen Beetle being the prime example (see our book *Volkswagen Car 1948-68*).

Consequently something was needed to break the mould, and Ford intended to do it by employing American styling on a small European car. During the latter part of 1958 a new, much disguised, small Ford first appeared on the roads and motoring correspondents got a hint that something revolutionary was about to appear.

Above: *Typical of Ford's publicity pictures of the 1960s, this view of the Anglia 123E (1,200cc), demonstrates the 'family attraction' of the small cars that Ford were producing for the new era.*

Even so, it was not until the new Anglia 105E appeared in Ford dealer's showrooms around the country in 1959, that the radical new style of the car became widely known. The car was equipped with an entirely new engine design, but both this and the drive train were features that were often overlooked in the press of the day. The reason for the lack of attention to the power unit was due to the car's radical body shape!

Yet the engine was both the heart and the success of a car that was to have nearly a nine-year production span! This was a four-cylinder overhead valve power plant with a greater bore size than stroke, and this enabled the car to have higher cruising speeds and belied the fact that its engine size was only 997cc.

Top Right: *Just right for those family days out, this Anglia 123E is seen by the two-furlong post at Carlisle Races. The full width chrome grille of the 123E makes a marked contrast with the more basic offering on the 105E seen below. The popularity of the Anglia range influenced a generation of drivers, many of whom went on to own either an Escort or a Cortina.* Alan Earnshaw

Middle Right: *Certainly less glamorous than the previous model, the 105E model in this picture is seen outside the David Brown Tractors factory near Huddersfield, with a youthful Alan Earnshaw at the wheel. It will be noticed that the car carries a two-tone paint scheme (Ermine White and Imperial Maroon), which was available as a factory finish at an extra cost.* Ellen Earnshaw

Bottom Right: *A late model 105E Anglia dating from 1967, this time a deluxe version, is seen in Huddersfield near an early model Escort, the car which superseded the Anglia.* Robert Berry.

The Anglia was quite revolutionary, with a completely new body and crisp angular lines that provided a compact two-door - four-seat saloon with really distinctive styling. This new body shape featured prominently and gave it what several commentators called 'a shark-like appearance'; primarily because the backward rake of the rear-screen looked like the dorsal fin of one of the denizens of the deep, though even the radiator grille continued the impression, with an almost mouth-like appearance.

With Alan's parents owning an Anglia between 1962 and 1965 he wrote, "I never saw such features in the car - but my wife (whilst still a schoolgirl) was knocked down by an Anglia 105E in 1964, and always maintained they had a 'vicious look'! Other people have unkindly referred to them as looking like a wide-mouthed frog. Be that as it may, the styling caught the public imagination and a place on an extended waiting list became the situation that many would-be owners found themselves in.

The headlights were mounted high into the top leading edge of the front wings and set under a slight cowl, whilst the bonnet swept gradually down between the wings onto the top of the low, wide radiator grille. On the deluxe model this grille was a chrome mesh structure, which extended to the triangular-shaped indicators at the very front corners of the wings, just above the bumpers. On the standard models, the grille was of thin, horizontal, body coloured slats that did not extend as far as the deluxe grille.

The rear wings were rather square, and though not amounting to the finned versions of the early-1960s American Fords, the origins were rather obvious. These 'fins' were accentuated by the downward sweep of the boot, which dropped between the two rear wings to meet the rather high sill that housed the number plate and the fuel filler (offset to the right). The rear of the wing 'fins' also housed the tail lights, but again it was the backward rake of the rear-screen that suggested the non-European styling.

Top Left: *With the introduction of the 123E model, the Anglia appealed instantly to buyers in a slightly higher market. Nevertheless it still had a low purchase price, good performance from a 1198cc four-cylinder engine and up-to-date styling.*

Middle Left: *Every form of styling very quickly dated in Europe, particularly so in Italy! After the initial sales of the Anglia proved to be very good, it lost its appeal in a very short time. The head of Ford in Italy consulted with Dagenham and it was agreed that the stylist Michelotti would be responsible for a new design of Anglia for the Italian market, thus the Torino was born.* Adrian Hall

Bottom Left: *The Ford Anglia models even got into uniform and proved so popular as 'Panda' cars that Ford produced a version especially for the British police forces.*

Basic models were painted in monotone colours, but the deluxe version was usually painted with a differently coloured roof; in addition a thin chrome strip ran along the waist. In August 1962 a Super version was introduced to the range with an 1198cc engine. It was appointed with almost identical appointments to the deluxe 105E, though there was one major external difference between the two models.

The new Super was also finished in the two-tone paint scheme as had been applied to the deluxe, but it also carried a full-length tapering flash along the waist as standard. This was usually finished in the same colour as the roof panel (though not always) and boarded by thin chrome strips. The model was also provided with badges displaying '1200 Super' on the boot lid. With the introduction of this more powerful version, the differentiating terms of 105E and 123E were applied, with the latter being given to the larger car.

The Anglia range was very popular from the outset, so it is not surprising that variations of the saloon were soon offered to an eager market. First came the estate cars, which were produced from 1961 until the last ones were made in late 1968. This was the followed by a small commercial van, the Thames 307E, which found a good deal of popularity with small businesses and fleet operators alike; who can fail to remember the large fleet of modified 307E models operated by Walls Ice Cream for instance. Less popular was the pick-up version and only a few of these were made, whilst the Anglia convertible was an almost non-existent species!

One very unique version of the Anglia was only encountered abroad, and even then, only in small numbers. This model was the Anglia Torino and was apparently developed at the suggestion of a certain F. M. Paradise, who was the head of Ford in Italy. Sales of the 105E had been very good at first, but the Italians were terribly fashion-conscious and after a while sales dropped away dramatically. So Ford agreed that a new body shell could be produced in Italy, but only on the proviso that it used as many of the 105E parts as possible.

The responsibility for the new design was given to the renowned stylist Michelotti, who submitted plans for a very fashionable vehicle. Whilst retaining the windscreen and doors of the 105E, the body was totally different forward of the screen and aft of the doors. The front of the car had a regular box-like profile with a level bonnet and wing line. The radiator grille consisted of seven fine chrome bars and had circular headlights set within it at each end; the whole being surrounded by a thin chrome band with small, rectangular sidelight and indicator light units below the grille, but above the plain bumper.

Production of the Anglia Torino was undertaken at the Officina Stampaggi Industriala (OSI) works in Turin between February 1965 and 1967. The cars were sold in Italy, Holland, and Belgium but were never officially imported into Britain. As far as the home market went, and despite the Anglia's popularity (as demonstrated by the continuing waiting lists), Ford decided to supersede it with a new model in 1967, when they almost at once reverted to a semi-bulbous shaped small saloon. Everyone thought the model was doomed to failure, and there were few waiting lists for the new car, but it surprised everyone and it was still with us 30 years on (after various transformations); it was of course the Ford Escort.

Ford moved boldly with their new car, and aimed at capturing the 'F' registration market when, for the first time since 1963, the registration suffix letter moved to commence on 1st August instead of New Year's Day. The Anglia models were quickly phased out, but rather surprisingly many of the later cars were turned-out in either a metallic gold or metallic blue finish. Among the last of the range to be built were a few estates, the production of these had to continue until the Escort estate was ready. Therefore a number of Anglia estates were still being registered as new with the 'G' plate of August 1968. Likewise the production of the 307E van continued into 1968, when they too were finally replaced with an Escort model, which like the Anglia is worthy of a book on its own.

Top Right: *Along with the Triumph Herald and the BMC Mini, the new Ford Anglias were the stars of the 1959 Motor Show. Such was the instant success of the Anglia that by 1961, estate cars were also introduced to the market. These were to remain in production until they were superseded by the first of the new Escort models in 1968.*

Middle Right: *Just in the same way that the 300E vans were built as commercial variants of the 100E Anglia and Prefect models, Ford replaced these with commercial versions of their new Anglia, these proved to be extremely popular throughout the country with a lot of prominent fleets taking examples.*

Bottom Right: *The Anglia 105E and 123E models proved to be very successful cars with well over 1,000,000 of them being sold. Here the very last leaves the production line, followed by the first*

THE CONSUL CLASSIC

Following quickly on from the rake-backed window of the Anglia, Ford decided to continue this styling concept in its new intermediate size car the Consul Classic. Placed neatly between the 997cc Anglia and 1703cc Consul 204E, the Consul Classic 315 burst on to the British motoring scene with a 1340cc OHV engine in 1961.

Aimed squarely as a smart family car it could seat four to five people in comfort, and there was a choice of two- or four-door models; the latter being most urgently needed (as we have already seen). The four-cylinder engine was basically an enlarged version of that used in the Anglia, whilst the four-speed gearbox offered an optional floor-mounted gear lever to the standard column change.

Above: *Like the Anglia, the backward sweep of the rear screen was the car's most pronounced feature, but the Classic also had a number of other novel styling features. Four headlights were incorporated into the design, with the wing and bonnet line slightly hooded over them.*

The profile of the Classic was designed in the American vogue to reflect speed-styling, a feature achieved by subtle use of swage lines and body panel pressing. The bonnet was forward-hinged, with the central portion sweeping down to a very low radiator grille between the headlights. The grille had five, four-pointed stars set within, and was mounted directly above a plain bumper, beneath which was a further portion of the radiator grille in the form of a small crescent shaped area.

Top Right: *The deluxe version was available in six duo-tone colours, with the roof being different to the body colour. The body colours were, like the Anglia deluxe, Windsor Grey, Imperial Maroon or Ambassador Blue (all with Ascot Grey as the contrast colour), or Aqua Blue, Lime Green, or Ascot Grey with Ermine White as the contrast.*

Middle Right: *The standard model was available in ten single tone colours, Ascot Grey, Windsor Grey, Savoy Black, Aqua Blue, Ambassador Blue, Lime Green, Goodwood Green, Panama Yellow, Ermine White, and Imperial Maroon. The latter being the colour of the two-door car (76 VMB) into which Alan Earnshaw is seen entering in 1965.* Ellen Earnshaw

Bottom Right: *This view of a Classic is taken this time outside the Huddersfield Friendly & Trades Club, showing a four-door saloon in Imperial Maroon and Grey.* Robert Berry

Internally the car was appointed with the luxuries normally to be expected from the Consul range. Deluxe versions of the car featured additional instrumentation as well as a full-circle chrome-plated horn ring on the steering wheel. The windscreen wipers were electrically-operated, as opposed to the traditional vacuum drive long associated with Fords (though many of the early Classic models were plagued by repetitive failures to the wiper motors). Another unusual feature of the wiper system was that the wipers were actually twin-bladed.

The Consul Classic had a dry weight of 18-cwt, a turning circle of 34 feet and Girling hydraulic brakes. Suspension was again with the Macpherson strut system at the front end, whilst semi-elliptical leaf springs were found at the rear. Steering was by Burman Re-circulating Ball and a three-piece track rod. All of this should have made for a more than satisfactory car to suit the needs of the average family, but something was sadly wrong!

The Classic seemed plagued by persistent engine defects, which received much adverse comment in the motoring press of the day. By 1962 the situation had become so bad, that Ford announced it was introducing a new, re-styled 1500cc engine. As part of the drive to regain customer confidence, Ford improved the range with some subtle changes as the 1340cc version became the 109E and the 1500c engine cars became the 116E.

No estate cars or convertible versions were ever officially produced, although there were unofficial conversions. Sadly, the Classic had not been the success Ford had hoped for and this new flagship of family motoring was destined to flounder by the end of 1963 in preference to the Cortina, which was rapidly developed to use both the 1500cc engine and a number of other components from the Classic. In the end only 84,694 1340cc versions were built, with even fewer (26,531) 1500cc models taking to the road! As stated earlier, my family had both versions, and I had the rare Lotus model (UVH 21) - they are sadly missed.

THE CONSUL CLASSIC CAPRI

The Ford Classic saloon had only been in production a few months when the company's range was further expanded by the introduction of a smart little sports coupe version. It was something of a departure from traditional Dagenham products, for never before had Ford of Great Britain produced what can only be described as a 2+2 seater coupe. The mechanical specification was almost identical to the Classic saloon, and the few variations that were evident were of an extremely minor nature.

It was the body styling that differed, but even then the overall weight was around the same 18-cwt mark. The improved air-smoothed shape gave the coupe an edge of an extra one to two miles per hour over its sister, along with marginally better fuel consumption. Below the waist line, the cars were again almost identical with the two-door version of the saloon, but it was above where the major differences were immediately noticed.

Above: *This Essex registered Consul Classic Capri is another Ford demonstrator, and the picture is obviously posed to reflect the luxurious life-style that this car would introduce its owners to.*

Both cars had the double curvature to the windscreen, but the Capri had a lower roof-line that swept gently down to a rear screen which was both wide and curved. This screen was set at an angle of some 40 degrees to the horizontal, thus making it a complete contrast to the rear-sweep of the back windows on the Classic. It was possible to have a long open area to the side of the cabin, as not only did the door windows wind fully down, so too did the small triangular windows to the rear of the door.

The windows actually wound down in a clockwise or anti-clockwise direction depending on your point of view, so that the vertical edge/frame of the window lay horizontally along the lower windowsill, leaving just the small quarter-light on the door showing.

Top Right: *Here we have another original publicity view of the Consul Classic Capri taken around the same time and location as the previous shot. Precisely where this picture was taken is not recorded in the Ford Library, but it is believed to be alongside the River Thames in Berkshire.*

Middle Right: *It is very surprising how few people who acquire a new car (or otherwise for that matter), fail to appreciate the very many different styling features that the designer incorporates to make the whole vehicle. After all the automobile is as much a three-dimensional art form as a mode of transport. This close-up of the off-side rear wing of a Classic Capri GT proves the point.*

Bottom Right: *Around 10-years old at the time this picture was taken, 315 HAJ is seen at Bradley in West Yorkshire. By this time a new breed of Capri had already come onto the market. These newer Fords, although bearing the same name, had very little in common with the Consul Classic Capri. However these later cars themselves have gone on to become highly sought after classics and have a wide following amongst Ford enthusiasts. By way of comparison, whilst the Consul Classic Capri has survived, it has done so in far fewer numbers.* Robert Berry

The roof-line of the car was a good two inches lower than the Classic saloon, a feat achieved by interior alterations and a lowering of the front seats. There was a bench-type seat in the back, which whilst satisfactory for small children was barely sufficient for two adults and no use at all for courting! In reality, the Capri was intended as a two-seater, the back bench was just that, although the manufacturers did offer the 'luxury' of a cushion to cover the platform as an optional extra.

The Capri was only available in the deluxe version, and as a result the coupe had some luxurious appointments. Over-riders were usually fitted as standard to the bumpers, whilst bright wheel trims and white-wall tyres were available as an extra. The interiors were fitted with a PVC lining covering a fibre-matting sound-proof material. The floor was fitted with a bri-Nylon carpet and the front seats were larger and contained more padding than those in the Classic. Some were even trimmed with leather, but the majority were in two-tone PVC to reflect the car's external colour scheme.

The seats were forward-hinged, using the frames of the seats employed on the two-door Classic, thus allowing access to the confined back 'seat' area. Like the Classic it was also re-equipped with a 1500cc engine in 1962, after which the 1340cc version went out of production, the total number built being 11,143. The 1500 stayed in production until 1964, during which time 7,573 models were built. A 1500 GT model was soon made available, but only 2,002 cars of this high-performance version were produced: however, those which took to the road were capable of upwards of 95mph in the days before the national speed limit was set at 60/70mph.

FORD ZEPHYR 4, ZEPHYR 6 AND ZODIAC MkIII

As noted in the section dealing with the MkII Consul, Zephyr and Zodiac models, Ford developed its plans for the large car market around a new body shell design, which was to be available as the Zephyr 4, Zephyr 6 and the Zodiac MkIII from 1962 onwards. However the Consul, a name that had been with us since 1956, was now missing from the range!

Also gone were the dazzling two-tone colour schemes of the earlier Zodiacs. Now, it was believed that the new models should primarily rely on a quiet dignity, an air of reserved elegance, which it was felt would appeal more to the discerning market.

Above: *Again representing the luxurious life-style that could come with Ford ownership, this picture shows a left-hand drive Zodiac MkIII outside the Casino at Monte Carlo.*

Having already made plans for a mid-range model, it was felt possible to move the whole of the new MkIII model range of large Fords more up-market. Yet, at the same time they decided to retain (with suitable modifications), the drive-train of the earlier models. There were still to be three models in the big car line-up, but the Consul name was cascaded from the large car range down to the family saloon market that was to be launched with the soon to be announced Classic.

Top Right: *In view of the fact that the name Zephyr had long been associated with Ford's larger offerings, this obviously donated a little extra panache to the new family saloons (and undoubtedly influenced a few sales as a result). A late model Zephyr 4, re-registered with a 'J plate' is seen in the company of an ex-GPO Morris 1000 van and a MkI Escort at Birkby, Huddersfield, in the early 1970s. The white stripe and painted bumper are not authentic!* Robert Berry

Middle Right: *Now preserved, this MkIII Zephyr 4 is pictured just off Blackwell Road in Carlisle and it shows off the rear aspect to good effect. The stylish wings and light clusters were a distinctive feature of the back view, whilst the rear registration plate concealed the fuel filler cap.* Alan Earnshaw

Bottom Right: *This 1966-registered Zephyr 4 also displays its classic lines whilst standing at the edge of Newton Cap Bank, near Bishop Auckland in the early-1970s.* Robert Berry

The modification of the over-head valve 1703cc in-line four-cylinder unit that had powered the MkII Consul was used in one of the new large models that were being introduced; this car was the Zephyr 4. The former six-cylinder engines of the Zephyr MkII and the Zodiac were also modified, and these were fitted into the new models that became known as the Zephyr 6 and the Zodiac MkIII. Actually, the new Zodiac was to have its own individuality as an executive model rather than be a luxury version of the Zephyr as before. They were then designated as model codes 211E (four-cylinder cars) and 213E (six-cylinder cars).

The new body design had been originally created by the elite Italian styling house of FRUA, but alterations to their designs were incorporated into the front end by the Canadian stylist Roy Brown; although the rear of the car remained largely to the FRUA design. The cars shared a similar design concept, but they had a unique radiator grille for each model, whilst the Zodiac also had a different layout in the rear passenger accommodation area. The styling of the cars was both totally different from earlier models and something of a compromise between Italian and American fashions.

These styling considerations resulted in a long, low and wide block-shaped car, with an airy cabin of full width screens. It was, in effect, a merging of lines from the prominent splayed rear wings, from where the eye could discern a styling line straight along the base of the side windows that ended at the leading outer edge of the large bonnet. From the point of the subtly rounded corner on the front wing, the body moulding returned back to be absorbed into the rear wing.

The bonnet and roof panel were rather flat and separated by a wide, nicely raked windscreen of double curvature between the two slender pillars. With the curved side windows, these pillars were a major consideration and they gave greater interior space and a very light and airy interior that in turn offered excellent visibility.

Top Left: *For the 1960s this MkIII Zephyr had instant 'Six Appeal', a blend of Italian and American styling with the power of a 2.5 litre six-cylinder engine. This ensured that Ford had got it all right again, as seen in this pre-launch picture.*

Middle Left: *The Zephyr Six proved to be a popular model for various police forces in Britain during the 1960s both in conventional saloon car form and the estate car versions, which had the Zodiac engine fitted. Who can fail to remember the BBC TV series* Z Cars, *in which great actors like Stratford Johns, Frank Windsor and Brian Blessed were amongst the stars?*

Bottom Left: *Ford's top MkIII model still wore the Zodiac badge, but later in the decade this was eclipsed by their fully equipped executive model.*

The rear doors on both Zephyr models incorporated a quarter-light behind the side window, and the rear roof pillar was noticeably wide. Meanwhile, on the Zodiac models, the rear door window was rather square and a small, triangular-shaped (non-opening) quarter light was a feature of the bodywork; whilst a slender rear roof pillar provided the Zodiac with a different rake and a little more glass area to its rear screen.

From an external rear view the Zodiac was different to the Zephyr, in as much as it featured full-width trim below its boot-lid that comprised of four thin chrome bands. At the front of the car, each model had its own style of radiator grille; that on the Zephyr 4 being a simple oblong of thin, concave vertical bars with its extreme outer edges on a slight diagonal outward taper on their climb towards the bonnet with the headlights set outside.

The Zephyr 6 had a radiator grille of a similar style but, being of full width, this appeared a little deeper and divided into two by a slender body-coloured 'V'; it also had the headlights situated within the outer ends of the radiator grille. The Zodiac wore a grille of a similar concave pattern but it was of a full width style representing fine vertical and horizontal bars. The Zodiac's illumination was in the form of dual headlights, but like the other models it had combined circular sidelight-indicator units in the lower front wing. The interior was upholstered in a new soft vinyl, though leather was an option at extra cost. The seats were of the bench type with central pull-down arm-rests, but individual front seats were also available. Internal door locks were of the push-down button type and the internal door release was a lever under the door-mounted arm-rest.

Reversing these big Fords was simplicity itself and although those angled rear fins housing the tail-light units were not to everyone's taste, they gave you something to aim with when negotiating a reverse manoeuvre between gateposts. Forward motion into a confined space was something else, and though you knew that there was a corner on your front wings, precisely where was anyone's guess!

A brilliant idea with these big Fords, after years of the infamous vacuum type windscreen wipes, was the introduction of a two-speed electric wiper. They actually move the rain, "I can see, I can see" one journalist wrote when they were tried out. What is more (and in the same review he wrote), "with all that sheet steel forward of the windscreen, we got the sensation of piloting the *Ark Royal* around Scarborough's boating lake." Underneath this vast steel sheet, which those who knew better called the bonnet, was the last variation of the 2,553cc straight-six engine, but in four years time the big Fords were to be powered by 'V' engines. Incidentally, a new four-speed gearbox was fitted to the MkIII models with synchromesh on all gears now, or if preferred the Borg-Warner automatic transmission. Various controls and warning lights were in front of the driver on a wide, mock-wood panel with the direction indicator and main beam warning lights, fuel and temperature gauges housed (with the speedometer) in a low, wide shroud above.

The well respected coach-builder, Hooper offered a really luxurious version of the Zodiac, this model, having extensive sound insulation, a fully re-trimmed interior, deep-pile quality carpets, and a choice of seats. Although retaining the same instrumentation of production Zodiac the dashboard was now veneered; Burr Walnut was used for this fascia and also for the matching door cappings. To complete the conversion, the boot was carpeted and the car was resprayed to the customer's individual choice of colour.

Ford produced their own flagship in the MkIII line-up in January 1965 and called the car the Zodiac Executive, basically the normal model but with every option fitted as standard equipment. One final (if somewhat sombre) variation was by the Bolton-based specialist coach-builders Coleman-Milne, who offered the Cardinal - a rather elegant hearse based on either of the two Zephyrs or the Zodiac.

Top Right: *No convertible models were offered on the MkIII, and although an estate car version had been absent when the new Zephyr and Zodiac first appeared in April 1962, by October this had been addressed. This being done by the traditional Ford estate car manufacturer Abbott's of Farnham who redressed this deficit and produced a very attractive conversion.*

Middle Right: *As our pictures on this page show, viewed from any angle, the MkII estates had the look of a genuinely planned model rather than the appearance of a converted saloon car. However, the prototype model had used a steel tailgate, whilst the production models utilised a fibreglass one.*

Bottom Right: *Although the Zodiac had a unique design to its latter cabin area, the Zephyr 6 and 4 models shared the same body. Yet even with the rather broad rear pillars, the Zephyr models too could boast a light and airy cabin area. All three models had their own style of radiator grill as illustrated in this official photograph of an early Zephyr 4 model.*

THE CONSUL CORTINA MkI

The year 1962 saw the launch of the Consul Cortina, which, although designed to replace the troubled Classic was eventually to become both one of Ford's best selling British models and a very long-running Marque. It was everything the Classic promised to be, a medium sized family car at a reasonable price, and excelling in its reliability - perhaps the only exception being poor starting on cold mornings! This was a little quirk that they became famous for, and one that gave us many a short hard run as we endeavoured to launch our mutual friend Brian Kenyon off to work at the local Co-op.

Except for this little idiosyncrasy, there were few teething problems for the front-engine - rear wheel drive car, as its power unit had been thoroughly tested in the latter models of the Consul Classic.

Above: *Ultimately the Cortina became the most successful British car range Ford ever built. The changes that were progressively introduced by Ford in these 20 years were undoubtedly a major part of the golden years of motoring.*

Considering the fact that its main competition, namely the transverse-engine/front wheel drive BMC 1100 series, was already an outstanding success it seems strange that Ford stuck to rear-wheel drive; but they did and the model soon started outselling its rivals. It was available as either a two-door or a four-door saloon, or as an estate and there was also a choice of engines, either 1200cc or 1500cc. The styling was relatively conventional, particularly when compared to the Classic, but this was probably intentional. The driver looked through a slightly curved windscreen, down to a low, wide radiator grille that reached almost to the sides of the car.

Top Right: *Clearly seen from this studio picture, the Cortina's bonnet featured a low wide hump, and a badge was fitted to this on its leading edge. On earlier models this proclaimed the car to be a Consul, but on later models it was changed to Cortina, was this again a desire to disassociate the car with its fore-runner?*

Middle Right: *Like the view above, this is an early production Cortina picture! Yet if you look twice, you will see that it is not the same car as above, despite the fact that the registration plate is identical on both models. The front aspect shown above is on a Super model with the chrome side trim, whilst the picture below shows the rear aspect of a GT version, as demonstrated by the 'Grand Tourer' badge on the rear wing. This picture also shows to good effect the circular tail light cluster, which was divided into three sections - indicator, reflector, and side/brake lights.*

Bottom Right: *A feature on the sides of the early Cortina super estate cars was this imitation wood trim, which was another American styling fad. For some reason this did not really appeal to the Cortina customer, but this feature rather set these models apart from other British estate cars and offered an individual look. By 1964 this was discontinued, after which the super estate was finished similar to the other models.*

On basic models the grille was formed from thin horizontal bars painted body colour, whilst the deluxe and super models had a chrome-mesh grille. Up to 1965 the oval sidelights located below the headlights were in the leading edge of the wings; however, the discontinuation of the basic model in that year led to a re-styled grille, which embraced the sidelights. The rear of the car had a deep and spacious boot that was fitted with a rather flat lid.

It was with a degree of trepidation that the circular rear lights, with their three pronged lens divisions were fitted to the cars at all, as it was feared that the public might associate them with Mercedes Benz cars from Germany. As things turned out the tri-divided circle actually became identified with the Campaign for Nuclear Disarmament, so another first for Ford was their subconsciously producing the first 'Politically Correct' car. The rear window was rather deep and full width giving excellent rear-vision. Chrome bumpers were fitted front and rear.

In 1962 a two-door coupe version, the prototype of which was sent to Ford in America for evaluation. Appropriately known as the Saxon, this stylish little car would have filled a much needed gap in the American small car market, but it was never put into production and some have commented that this was due to Detroit's 'not invented here' attitude. The following year GT models were introduced to the UK in both the four-door and two-door versions; these had a standard Cortina 1500cc over-head valve engine, but were fitted with a Webber carburettor that increased the output to 83 brake-horse power. Naturally the GT models were also given additional appointments, including a luxury interior.

Top Left: *Whereas estate versions of pre-1960s Ford models had relied on outside conversions, the Anglia 105E had shown that Ford could produce and market a successful range of factory-built models. Such an option had not been available for the Classic, but the Cortina resumed the mantle. The estate cars had heavy-duty rear suspension and a one-piece tailgate that made it necessary to change the large circular tail lights to a vertical styled lamp unit, which was worn on the end of the rear wings. All the estate cars had a cabin-like extended saloon, indeed the rear-most roof pillar on them was very similar to that on the saloon.*

Middle Left: *To cater for the motorist who wanted a car with increased performance, Ford introduced the GT version of the Cortina; this version is illustrated here by this model finished in Ermine white with the discrete badge on the rear flank. The Grand tourer versions were fitted with the 1500cc OHV engine, but had a webber carburettor to increase performance. These models were available in either two- or four-door saloon models and were given additional appointments, including a more luxurious interior.*

Bottom Left: *This 1964 model shows the revised radiator grille, which was incorporated into the sidelight/indicator unit; if the reader looks back to the top photograph on page 47 they will notice the subtle change. The 1500 super model featured here (available in two- door or four-door form), also serves to show how the concave side flash was finished with chrome trim on the top of the range Cortina models at this time; often this flash was also painted in the contrasting colour that was used on the roof. .*

By February 1963 Ford had developed an arrangement with Lotus to produce a sports car version of the Cortina, after this well-known sports car manufacturer had experimented with a number of Classic models (believed to be 12 in all). It was one of these twelve in which one of your authors experienced a pile-up at Leicester in 1969, what a waste. This semi-official trial with the Classic paved the way for marrying together the Cortina body-shell and the Lotus 105bhp engine. Approximately 3,301 Lotus models were made between 1963 and 1966, though this was only a small proportion of the total Cortina MkI production that lasted until the introduction of the MkII model in 1966.

By the time of the Earls Court Motor Show in 1963 there were 12 models in the Cortina line-up from the basic two-door saloon selling at £573 to the Lotus Cortina which had a price tag of £1,100. Besides the various saloon cars already mentioned, three estate cars arrived upon the scene in March 1963; these were the 1200 De-luxe, the 1500 De-luxe and the Super.

Crayford, the convertible specialists, did not work on many MkI Cortinas as they were very busy with conversions on other cars and an order for '57 Varieties' of the Mini-based Wolseley Hornet convertible.

Incidentally, these Minis were painted either 'Toga White or Birch Grey' and were prizes in one of the largest consumer competitions of 1966, which was organised by one of the country's biggest food manufacturers. As usual, Crayford made an excellent job of the Ford Cortina although it is thought that only a handful were converted for the British market before the MkI Cortina was succeeded by the MkII. However, besides the home market conversions, around 30 were built for use as taxis and exported to Bermuda.

Crayford also went on to make convertibles of each Ford Cortina from the MkI to the MkV, as each model succeeded the previous one. It is rumoured that among the MkII conversions, 20 of them were of the Lotus version. Finally, as far as our time period is concerned, this was the end of the Cortina story. Yet, the car's drive-train was continued (at first) in the totally re-styled MkII which appeared in 1966. As we will tell in a later book, this MkII model had a much more squared appearance!

The MkII models also went on to employ either a 1300 or 1600 engine. Yet, this was only the second variant in a Marque that continued for over a quarter of a century until the Ford Sierra eventually replaced the Mk. V Cortina, the last of the breed in July 1982, The original Ford Cortina appeared in the autumn of 1962, and when production ended no fewer than 4,279,079 had been built.

Below: *The Cortina family circa 1964 pictured in an official photograph, which besides revealing the photographer's shadow, also shows the two-door, four-door and estate versions of a car that became a market leader. The Ford Cortina had been named after the location of the 1960 winter Olympic sports in Italy at Cortina d' Ampezzo to give the new family saloon an 'international air'. The models were certainly enthusiastically welcomed by the car-buying British public, which encouraged the Ford Motor Company to offer more variants of the Cortina than any model previously manufactured by them.*

THE CONSUL CORSAIR

Although the Corsair was developed towards the end of the period that our book is concerned with, and not particularly well-represented in preservation, it was in danger of becoming the forgotten Fords!

Robert Berry well recalls their arrival however, writing: "The very first time I saw one, I was ten years old at the time, it was at the junction of a busy road in Huddersfield. I remember it as being a beautiful car, pale green with a cream roof, and I recall being very impressed as I watched it drive away. When my father and I had walked into the town centre, we stopped and admired others in the showroom of the main dealers, Brockholes Motor Company."

It was at the Motor Show in October 1963 that the Ford Consul Corsair, first appeared. By this time the Consul name was being used as the entry-level to the big Fords, as it was considered a little down-market, so it was attached to the early Cortina and Corsair models but was soon deleted. The Ford Motor Company then, as now, wanted to build cars for everyone and the Corsair was aimed at customers who wanted something a little more up-market than the Cortina but did not want a car as large as the Zephyr.

Above: *The styling of the Corsair, was in truth nothing ultra-exciting, but it did have a crisp and clean style possessing a certain harmony. This was accentuated in the way that the top wing line and bonnet swept gently down to the shallow wide radiator grille with it's slightly recessed headlights; while the bottom wing line almost mirrored the curve on it's way up. The overall styling was rather reminiscent of the 1961 Ford Thunderbird, and it may have been slightly influenced by USA fashion, but it was much less extreme. From 1963 until 1965, the model range consisted of the Corsair 120E and the Corsair GT, both of which were available as either two- or four-door saloon cars. Cars that were finished in one of the two-tone schemes had a greater emphasis of style due to the broad rear pillar.*

Originally, all the Corsairs had a 1,498cc straight four-cylinder engine with over-head valves, the bore and stroke being 80.97mm x 72.75mm. As with all Fords at this time, the Macpherson strut suspension system was used at the front, while the rear end employed semi-elliptic springs. Disc brakes of 9.5" were used at the front of the cars, while the rear wheels were fitted with 9" drum brakes.

Top Right: *Ford decided to give each range an executive model during the 1960s, and top of the Corsair range was the luxurious 2000E; among the external features was the vinyl roof covering.*

Middle Right: *The GT models were fitted with a high performance version of the 1,498cc engine, in which the principle changes were a four-branch aluminium inlet manifold. They were fitted with a dual-barrel Weber carburettor as opposed to the single-barrel Zenith of the standard engine, and they also had larger exhaust valves and re-shaped combustion chambers.*

Bottom Right: *During 1966 our old friends, Abbot's of Farnham, turned their attention to estate car conversions of the Corsair with the full approval of the Ford Motor Company.*

In 1965 Ford switched to V4 engines to power the Corsair, and after this customers had a choice of either 1,700cc or a two-litre engine; as a matter of interest, the Corsair's with the V4 engine had bigger front disc brakes too.

To capture every sector of the market, Ford needed an executive car in every model range during the late 1960s; for example the Escort 1300E, and the MkII Cortina 1600E, so it came as no great surprise when in January 1967 the Corsair range received it's own flagship in the form of the Corsair 2000E. Although outside our time-scale we might still mention that this variant was quite lavishly appointed with its engine and luggage compartment lights, deeply upholstered reclining bucket seats, Nylon deep-pile carpeting, built-in push-button radio, walnut fascia and fully carpeted boot. Obvious external differences were the black vinyl roof, fancy road wheel covers and a new radiator grille of thin horizontal bars.

As with other Corsair models, Girling disc and drum brakes were fitted, as the big engine (with it's Weber down-draught Carburettor) could accelerate the car from 0-60 in 12.5 seconds. Bodywork was usually painted in one of the shades of metallic paint that were becoming increasingly popular, giving the 2000E an even more up-market appeal. In all its various forms, the Corsair sold rather well through its years, but it was quietly withdrawn from the Ford range when the Cortina MkIII was introduced. This new, larger Cortina, provided models that had been offered in the Cortina MkII and the Corsair ranges, but from now on economies of manufacturing could be more readily achieved with just one basic body pressing.

There you have the case for the defence but, as with all cars, the Corsair has not escaped criticism. For instance, the top of the front wings would rust through on badly neglected cars, and lets face it, the early V4 engine was not without fault. Yet, on the whole, the Corsair was quite a good car, no scorcher, but then again it was never intended to be. It was just one of the reliable family saloons that Ford had continued to offer to the public, based on overall levels of research, design and mass production, followed by sales and service and customer support from a network of dealers which other manufacturers would have been proud to offer!

ACKNOWLEDGMENTS

This fully-revised edition of our original book has been produced to meet the demands of readers as the original volume has long since been out of print, but has been re-issued by popular demand. That original book was produced with the very kind support of Simon Sproule, then based in Ford's Corporate Affairs Department. Other willing contributors included Ron Staughton of the Dagenham Heritage Centre and Fran Camberlain of Ford's photographic department.

This new edition reflects a number of minor changes that have been advised by the various Ford owner's clubs, and we are more than grateful for their kindness and support. Also, through the extremely kind services of the Ford Motor Company we have had the good fortune to revise and improve the photographic contents of this edition. We sincerely hope that you enjoy the results.

Above: *Anglia bodyshells stand on skid units, having been painted - look out for our forthcoming book on this fascinating model from the Ford range.*

Special thanks are extended to:

The Ford Motor Company.
Various Ford Owners Clubs,
Larraine Earnshaw,
Adrian Hall,
Dave Hill,
Aidan Quigley,
Colin Moorhouse,
Claire Newton,
Matthew & Bryony Richardson, and
Louise Tarn.